Welcome to the captivating
where lightning reflexes ar
on a table just a few centim

50 Legends of Table Tennis" is a vibrant tribute
to these masters of table tennis, athletes whose
agility and precision have redefined what it
means to be a champion.

From the hypnotic sound of the ball bouncing off
the table to the epic duels that have captivated
global audiences, this book is a thrilling
exploration of the lives, struggles and triumphs
of those who have elevated table tennis to an art
form.

Join us on this journey through the history of this
exhilarating sport, and discover the stories
behind the names that have shaped its legend.

SUMMARY

SUMMARY

WANG LIQIN

BORN JUNE 18, 1978 IN SHANGHAI, CHINA

A three-time world champion, Wang Liqin dominated the tables with remarkable skill and precision. His career is also marked by two gold medals in men's doubles at the Olympic Games, and a bronze medal in singles in 2004. Wang Liqin was world number one for several long periods.

THE TITAN OF PING-PONG: THE HEGEMONY OF WANG LIQIN

Wang Liqin is famous for his powerful and aggressive style of play, combined with excellent ball-handling technique. He stands out for his ability to generate devastating topspins, which have often left his opponents helpless. His imposing stature, combined with his speed and precision, allowed him to dominate world ping pong for a decade.

Wang Liqin left his mark on the history of ping-pong with several notable events. In addition to his world titles, he was a pillar of the Chinese team, contributing to its hegemony in the sport. His rivalry with other great players such as Ma Lin and Jan-Ove Waldner captivated fans, providing memorable matches and boosting global interest in ping pong. Away from the tables, Wang Liqin is committed to the development of sport in China, playing a crucial role in the training of young talents. His transition from player to coach was a turning point, showing his dedication and lasting impact on the sport. His approach to the game, characterized by in-depth tactical analysis and rigorous mental preparation, was a source of inspiration for future generations.

Wang Liqin has owned more than 10 types of personalized rackets."

MA LONG, "THE DRAGON"

BORN OCTOBER 20, 1988, ANSHAN, LIAONING, CHINA

Ma Long has won the World Singles Championships three times, and won Olympic singles gold at Rio 2016 and Tokyo 2020. Ma Long also contributed significantly to the Chinese team's successes, winning several gold medals. team gold at the Olympic Games and World Championships.

THE PING-PONG MAESTRO AND HIS LEGENDARY TRAJECTORY

Ma Long's fame is based on his impeccable technique, his mental strength and his ability to dominate the most prestigious competitions. His unique racquet grip, exceptionally powerful backhand and aggressive attacking game set him apart from his competitors. Ma Long is famous for his ability to remain calm under pressure, a quality that has earned him many major titles.

Ma Long left his mark on the history of ping-pong with his remarkable career. His back-to-back singles victories at the World Championships and two Olympic singles gold medals illustrate his undisputed dominance. Outside of competitions, Ma Long is a mentor and role model for young players, contributing to the development of ping pong in China and around the world. His commitment to the sport goes beyond his individual performances, as evidenced by his key role in China's team victories. His showdowns with other great players, like Zhang Jike and Xu Xin, were standout moments, delivering epic duels that captivated fans around the world. Finally, his longevity and his ability to remain at the top despite changes in the sport and the rise of new talents are testament to his exceptional career.

He is the first male Olympic champion for the second consecutive time in table tennis.

JAN-OVE WALDNER
"MOZART OF PING-PONG"

BORN OCTOBER 3, 1965 IN STOCKHOLM, SWEDEN

His career is marked by notable successes, including winning gold at the 1992 Olympic Games in singles and silver in 2000. Jan-Ove Waldner won the World Championships in singles in 1989 and 1997, and was a finalist at three more times. Waldner also shone in doubles and teams.

THE SWEDISH VIRTUOSO WHO REDEFINED PING-PONG

Jan-Ove Waldner is famous for his unparalleled technical mastery and game intelligence. His ability to read the game and anticipate his opponents' moves was almost magical, hence his nickname "Mozart of Ping-Pong". Waldner was known for his varied and unpredictable play, skillfully combining offense and defense. His popularity has transcended borders, particularly in China, where he has gained immense popularity, something rare for a non-Chinese player.

Jan-Ove Waldner's career has been marked by many notable events. His triumph at the 1992 Olympic Games in Barcelona remains an iconic moment, where he demonstrated overwhelming superiority, not losing a single set during the tournament. Waldner played a crucial role in Sweden's emergence as a major force in global table tennis, breaking China's dominance in the 1980s and 1990s. His sporting longevity is also notable; he has maintained a high level of performance well beyond the typical retirement age in elite sport. His popularity in China reached such a level that a stamp bearing his image was issued there in 1997, a rare honor for a foreign athlete. Waldner has also been an ambassador for the sport, promoting ping pong across the world and inspiring many generations of players.

A Chinese stamp bearing his image was issued in 1997.

ZHANG JIKE

BORN FEBRUARY 16, 1988 IN QINGDAO, SHANDONG, CHINA

World singles champion in 2011 and 2013, Zhang Jike also won Olympic gold in singles at the 2012 London Games. His exceptional performance saw him complete the Grand Slam in a record time of 445 days, a remarkable feat in the sport.

THE BLAZING STAR OF CHINESE PING-PONG

Zhang Jike is famous for his dynamic playing style and his ability to dominate under pressure. His exceptional speed, power and precision allowed him to win against the best players in the world. He is particularly recognized for completing the Grand Slam of table tennis (world championships, World Cup, and Olympic gold medal) in record time, thus affirming his place among the legends of the sport.

Zhang Jike's career is punctuated by unforgettable moments. His triumph at the 2011 World Championships was a turning point, where he defeated big-name opponents, asserting his supremacy. His victory at the 2012 Olympics cemented his status as a sports superstar. Zhang Jike is also known for his unique celebrations after victories, including his famous "barrier destruction celebration", which captivated media and fans. Outside of his sporting career, he has engaged in various initiatives promoting ping pong and participated in charitable activities, showing his commitment to the sport and the community. His rivalry with other great players, such as Ma Long and Timo Boll, created legendary matches, contributing to the evolution and popularity of modern ping pong.

He is the seventh player in the world to achieve the Grand Slam in table tennis and does not use the pen grip but the classic racket grip.

DENG YAPING

BORN FEBRUARY 5, 1973 IN ZHENGZHOU, HENAN, CHINA

His career is marked by four Olympic gold medals, won at the Games in Barcelona in 1992 and Atlanta in 1996. Deng Yaping won six world titles in singles and doubles between 1989 and 1995. Deng dominated the world rankings for several years, asserting her position as an exceptional player.

THE LEGEND WHO OVERCAME BARRIERS

Deng Yaping is famous not only for his impressive track record, but also for breaking stereotypes in the world of ping pong. Despite his small size, often seen as a disadvantage in sport, Deng proved that technique, speed and strategy could overcome physical barriers. She is known for her fast play, precise ball touch and astonishing reflexes.

Deng Yaping overcame many obstacles to reach the pinnacle of world table tennis. She faced prejudice due to her small size, with many coaches and officials doubting her potential because of it. However, Deng defied all expectations, becoming one of the best players of all time. Her singles victory at the 1992 Olympics was a key moment, propelling her onto the international stage. Deng also played a crucial role in maintaining China's dominance in women's table tennis during the 1990s. Her retirement in 1997, while still at the top of her game, was a notable event, marking the end of an era. After her sporting career, Deng engaged in various initiatives, including sports promotion and education.

Deng Yaping was elected to the Table Tennis Hall of Fame in 2003.

KONG LINGHUI
"PING-PONG PRINCE"

BORN OCTOBER 18, 1975 IN HARBIN, HEILONGJIANG, CHINA

Kong Linghui was crowned Olympic champion in doubles in 1996 and singles in 2000, achieving a historic performance for his country. Kong also won the World Doubles Championships in 1995 and 1999, and was a key part of the Chinese team in international competitions.

THE MASTER OF PRECISION AND ELEGANCE

Kong Linghui is famous for his impeccable technique and elegant playing style. He was one of the rare players to excel in both singles and doubles, demonstrating exceptional versatility. His ability to deliver high-level performances in intense pressure situations has set him apart from his peers. Kong is also recognized for his fair play and exemplary behavior on and off the field, earning the respect of opponents and fans around the world.

Kong Linghui's career is full of memorable moments. His victory in singles at the Sydney Olympic Games in 2000 was an important milestone, establishing him as one of the best players in the history of Chinese table tennis. His successful doubles partnership with Liu Guoliang formed one of the most formidable pairs in the history of the sport. Kong also played a crucial role as a mentor and coach, helping to cultivate the next generation of ping pong champions in China. His move from player to coach was an example of a successful transition, showing his dedication and love for the sport. Kong has also been an ambassador for ping pong, promoting the game and its sportsmanship across the world.

At twelve years old, he was already a member of the Chinese national team. In 1994, he won his first individual title, the junior world championship.

LIU GUOLIANG

BORN JANUARY 10, 1976 IN XINXIANG, HENAN, CHINA

Olympic champion in singles in Atlanta in 1996 and in doubles in Sydney in 2000, Liu Guoliang also won the world doubles title in 1995 and 1999. Liu was one of the first players to complete the Grand Slam of ping-pong, a remarkable feat.

THE REVOLUTIONARY INNOVATOR OF PING-PONG

Liu Guoliang is famous for revolutionizing the game of ping pong with his unique style of attacking play. He was one of the first to master and popularize the backhand penhold technique, a major innovation in the sport. His aggression, coupled with exceptional technique, allowed Liu to dominate the sport in the 1990s. His ability to combine power and precision made him a formidable and respected player.

Liu Guoliang has left his mark on ping-pong with several notable achievements. Her singles victory at the 1996 Olympics was a historic moment, asserting her dominance in the sport. In doubles, his collaboration with Kong Linghui formed one of the most dynamic and victorious pairs in history. After his playing career, Liu became an influential coach, leading the Chinese national team to numerous international successes. Under his leadership, the Chinese table tennis team continued to dominate the world, reflecting his tactical expertise and ability to inspire subsequent generations. His role in the evolution of the game, both as a player and as a coach, left a lasting imprint on the sport.

he is the creator of the revolutionary penhold backhand technique.

GUO YUE

BORN JULY 17, 1988 IN ANSHAN, LIAONING, CHINA

Team gold medalist at the 2008 Olympic Games and singles bronze medalist in Beijing, Guo Yue has shone on the international stage from a young age. World singles champion in 2007, she also won several doubles and team world titles.

THE PRODIGIOUS PING-PONG CHAMPION

Guo Yue is famous for her rapid rise to the top of world women's table tennis. From a young age, she demonstrated exceptional talent and maturity, establishing herself as a dominant force. Her aggressive technique, combined with excellent mobility and powerful punches, set her apart from her competitors. Guo Yue is also known for her versatility, excelling in singles, doubles and team events.

Guo Yue's career is punctuated by remarkable moments. Her singles victory at the 2007 World Championships was a highlight, placing her among the sport's elite. Particularly impressive was her performance at the 2008 Beijing Olympics, where she helped the Chinese team win gold and took bronze in singles. Guo Yue stood out not only for her successes, but also for her ability to maintain high performance at a young age, competing with more experienced players. She also played a crucial role in maintaining China's supremacy in women's table tennis, inspiring many young players around the world. Her commitment and passion for the sport was evident in every match she played.

Guo Yue won his first major title at just 16 years old.

ZHANG YINING

BORN OCTOBER 5, 1981 IN BEIJING, CHINA

Zhang Yining is considered one of the greatest female ping pong players of all time. Her record includes four Olympic gold medals (two in singles in 2004 and 2008, and two in doubles in 2004 and 2008) and ten world champion titles (singles, doubles, and team) between 1999 and 2008.

THE UNDISPUTED QUEEN OF WORLD PING-PONG

Zhang Yining is famous for her absolute dominance in women's ping pong. Its ability to maintain world number one for an extended period is a testament to its technical and tactical superiority. She is known for her intelligent and strategic style of play, combining powerful shots with surgical precision. Her mastery of the top-spin and stroke game has distinguished her in international competitions.

Zhang Yining's career is punctuated by historic moments. Her performance at the 2004 and 2008 Olympic Games, where she won two gold medals each time, was a remarkable feat. She has maintained almost uninterrupted dominance in international competitions, often against equally talented opponents. Zhang played a crucial role in maintaining China's supremacy in women's table tennis. Her rivalry with other great players, like Wang Nan and Li Xiaoxia, provided some of the most captivating matches in sports history. Away from the table, Zhang has been an ambassador for ping pong, promoting the game across the world and inspiring generations of young players.

She was world number one for more than five consecutive years.

MA LIN

BORN FEBRUARY 19, 1980 IN SHENYANG, LIAONING, CHINA

Ma Lin won Olympic singles gold at the 2008 Beijing Games, as well as two doubles gold medals (2004 and 2008). At the world championship level, Ma Lin excelled, winning several singles, doubles and team titles.

THE SERVING VIRTUOSO AND KING OF OLYMPIC PING-PONG

Ma Lin is famous for his innovative playing style, especially his unique serving technique, often called "ghost serve", which has confused many opponents. He is also recognized for his excellent use of the pen hold, a less common technique at high levels, which he has mastered to perfection. His ability to generate unpredictable effects and his intelligent game strategy have made him a formidable and respected player.

Ma Lin marked the history of ping-pong with several notable achievements. Her Olympic Games victories in singles and doubles were highlight moments, demonstrating her ability to excel under intense pressure. His duel against Wang Hao in the 2008 Olympic final is an iconic example of his skill and fighting spirit. Additionally, Ma Lin was a key player in the Chinese team's victories at the world championships, contributing significantly to China's dominance in the sport. He is also known for his longevity in the sport, remaining competitive at a high level for many years. Outside of competitions, Ma Lin has been an ambassador for the sport, inspiring generations of players through his commitment and passion for ping pong.

Ma Lin has won four World Cups (2000, 2003, 2004 and 2006), more than any other player. A hell of a record!

#11

XU XIN, "SHOWMAN"

BORN JANUARY 8, 1990 IN XUZHOU, JIANGSU, CHINA

Xu Xin is one of the most accomplished ping pong players of his generation. His record includes several singles, doubles and team titles at the World Championships. He also won several gold medals at the Asian Championships and was a key player in the Chinese team's World Team Cup victories.

THE PING-PONG ARTIST WITH A MASTERFUL BACKHAND

Xu Xin is famous for his unique playing style and exceptional backhand, considered one of the best in the world. His ability to make incredibly creative shots and his strategic use of the playing space sets him apart from his competitors. Xu is also known for his excellent mobility and ability to return balls that would seem out of reach for most players.

Xu Xin's career is punctuated by many notable events. Particularly notable is his dominance in the doubles and team competitions, where he demonstrated an exceptional understanding of team play. Xu has played a crucial role in maintaining China's supremacy in global table tennis, especially in major international competitions. He is also known for his victories against some of the greatest ping pong players, including his own teammates on the Chinese team. Outside of the game, Xu is loved for his sportsmanlike attitude and positive interaction with fans and media, helping to promote the sport around the world.

Xu Xin is left-handed, making him a popular doubles partner. His game is based on a long and devastating top spin, both forehand and backhand

FAN ZHENDONG, "LITTLE FATTY"

BORN JANUARY 22, 1997 IN GUANGZHOU, GUANGDONG, CHINA

Fan Zhendong has won multiple titles at the World Championships, both in singles, doubles and teams. Fan also shone at the Asian Championships and has been a mainstay of the Chinese national team in numerous international competitions.

POWER AND PRECISION INCARNATE

Fan Zhendong is famous for his explosive strength and aggressive playing style. He is known for his ability to generate enormous power in his punches, while maintaining remarkable precision. Fan also stands out for his speed and responsiveness, which allows him to dominate his opponents in fast and intense exchanges.

Fan Zhendong's career has been marked by several exceptional moments. He quickly became a leading figure of the Chinese team, contributing significantly to its success in international competitions. Fan distinguished himself with his impressive victory at the World Championships, affirming his position among the world's ping pong elite. His rivalry with other great players, like Ma Long, led to legendary matches, full of tension and excitement. Outside of competitions, Fan is recognized for his hard work and dedication to the sport, serving as a role model for young players aspiring to reach the heights of ping pong.

Fan Zhendong is the record holder for World Cup singles victories. He has won five editions, respectively in 2016, 2018, 2019, 2020 and 2021.

TIM BALL

BORN MARCH 8, 1981 IN ERBACH IM ODENWALD, GERMANY

Timo Boll won several singles and doubles titles at the European Championships and was a major player in the German team's victories. Boll has also enjoyed success at the global level, with significant victories at the ITTF Opens and notable performances at the World Championships.

THE EUROPEAN MAESTRO OF PING-PONG

Timo Boll is famous for his exceptional technique and smooth attacking play. Recognized for his fair play and exemplary behavior, Boll is a respected figure in the world of ping-pong. He is notable for his ability to compete effectively with top Asian players, a notorious feat given Asia's dominance in the sport. His game is characterized by a great variation of shots, excellent hand-eye coordination.

Timo Boll's career has been marked by many remarkable events. He has been ranked among the best players in the world several times, a feat for a European player in a sport dominated by Asians. Boll won multiple European singles and team titles, asserting his position as a leader in European table tennis. His confrontations with legends of Chinese ping-pong, such as Ma Long and Zhang Jike, have gone down in history for their intensity and high technical level. Boll has also been an ambassador for the sport, promoting ping pong in Europe and internationally, and inspiring many young players.

Timo Boll started acting at the age of four. In 1986 he became a member of the TSV Höchst club, and he was spotted at the age of eight.

WANG HAO

BORN DECEMBER 15, 1983 IN CHANGCHUN, JILIN, CHINA

A three-time Olympic singles silver medalist, Wang Hao has won numerous world titles, both in singles, doubles and team events. His playing style, characterized by a reverse penholder grip and a powerful backhand, revolutionized modern ping pong. Wang Hao has dominated many international competitions.

THE INNOVATOR OF THE REVERSE PENHOLDER

Wang Hao is famous for having revolutionized the pen-hold backhand technique. He was one of the first players to effectively use the penhold backhand with such power and precision, changing the way this style is played. His ability to combine speed, power, and tactics made him formidable in competition. His series of Olympic silver medals testifies to his consistency at the highest level.

Wang Hao's career has been marked by his impressive performances at the Olympic Games and World Championships. Although he often came close to Olympic gold, his silver medals showed his perseverance and excellence in an extremely competitive sport. In addition to his individual successes, Wang Hao has been a key member of the Chinese national team, contributing to numerous team victories. After retiring, he became a coach, sharing his expertise and experience, and thereby influencing the next generation of ping pong players.

Wang Hao is known for his multiple defeats in the finals, in singles, of numerous world events. Thus he lost 2 finals of the World Championships against Zhang Jike (2011, 2013) but above all, he lost 3 finals of the Olympic Games in 2004 against the Korean Ryu Seung-min, in 2008 against his compatriot Ma Lin and against Zhang Jike in 2012 .

FENG TIANWEI

BORN AUGUST 31, 1986 IN HARBIN, HEILONGJIANG, CHINA

Feng Tianwei won the singles bronze medal at the 2012 London Olympics, after contributing to Singapore's team silver medal at the 2008 Beijing Games. Feng has also won multiple medals at the World Championships, especially as a team.

THE PILLAR OF SINGAPOREAN PING-PONG

Feng Tianwei is famous for putting Singaporean table tennis on the world stage. She is known for her determination and offensive style of play, characterized by quick shots and excellent counter-attacking technique. Its team victory at the 2008 Olympics was historic for Singapore, breaking decades of dominance by Chinese teams.

Feng Tianwei's career has been marked by significant victories and historic moments. His major contribution to Singapore's silver medal at the 2008 Olympic Games was a turning point for table tennis in his country. Feng has maintained a leadership position in the Singapore national team, regularly contributing to its success in international competitions. She beat several top Chinese players, a notable feat given China's dominance in the sport. In addition to his sporting successes, Feng is a role model for young athletes in Singapore, inspiring a new generation of ping pong players.

She won the team gold medal in 2010 at the World Table Tennis Team Championships at the expense of the Chinese team, which had been undefeated for 17 years in this competition.

CHEN MENG

BORN JANUARY 15, 1994 IN QINGDAO, SHANDONG, CHINA

The 2021 world singles champion, Chen Meng has also won several doubles and team titles at various international championships, including the ITTF World Championships and Opens. Chen has regularly topped the world rankings, demonstrating her supremacy in women's ping pong.

THE DOMINATRIX OF MODERN FEMALE PING-PONG

Chen Meng is famous for her dominance in women's ping pong. Her aggressive style of play, combined with impeccable technique, sets her apart from her opponents. She is particularly recognized for her ability to maintain high intensity throughout the match, which allows her to gain the upper hand over her opponents.

Chen Meng's career is punctuated by many notable events. His victory at the World Championship in 2021 was a key moment, affirming his status as a world leader. She also played a crucial role in China's team victories, contributing to its continued dominance in the sport. Her duels against other great players, like Ding Ning and Mima Ito, became classic clashes, showcasing her competitiveness and determination. In addition to her sporting successes, Chen is recognized for her hard work and dedication, serving as a role model for young athletes.

Chen Meng has won four consecutive China Open titles.

SUN YINGSHA

BORN ON NOVEMBER 4, 2000 IN SHIJIAZHUANG, HEBEI, CHINA

Sun Yingsha has won several major titles, including victories at the ITTF World Championships and Opens. Sun also played a crucial role in the Chinese team's success, contributing to doubles and team victories.

THE PRODIGIOUS RISE OF A PING-PONG STAR

Sun Yingsha is famous for his meteoric rise in the world of ping pong. She stands out for her aggressive play, her speed of execution and her ability to deliver powerful blows. Her technique and tactics of play, combined with her combative temperament, allowed her to quickly establish herself as one of the best players in the world.

Sun Yingsha's career is marked by several notable events. She established herself as a key player for the Chinese team, winning important titles in various international tournaments. His dynamic playing style and fighting spirit have earned him remarkable victories against top opponents. Sun has also demonstrated impressive maturity and resilience for his young age, adapting quickly to the pressures of high-level sport. His performances in the team and doubles competitions were also crucial, showing his ability to work as a team and contribute to collective success.

She becomes world singles champion in 2023. She also won the mixed doubles title with Wang Chuqin.

WANG NAN

BORN OCTOBER 23, 1978 IN FUSHUN, LIAONING, CHINA

Wang Nan won four Olympic gold medals and was a multiple-time world champion in singles, doubles, and teams. Wang Nan dominated women's ping pong in the 2000s, distinguishing herself with her offensive play, precise technique and ability to excel under pressure.

THE EMPRESS OF WORLD PING-PONG

Wang Nan is famous for her versatile playing style and dominance in women's ping pong. She is known for her excellent ball control, her keen tactical sense and her ability to maintain pressure on her opponents. Wang was a key figure in China's dominance in women's table tennis, helping to establish the country as a superpower in the sport.

Wang Nan's career is marked by historic moments and milestone victories. His Olympic gold medals, especially those won in singles, proved his supremacy in the sport. Wang was also a formidable opponent in doubles and team play, demonstrating an excellent understanding of team play. Her ability to stay at the top of the world rankings for an extended period of time and beat the best players of her generation cemented her reputation as a ping pong legend. Aside from her sporting successes, Wang has been an inspiration to many young female players, in China and around the world.

She was the first player to win Olympic gold in both singles and doubles.

VIKTOR BROWN

BORN AUGUST 24, 1911 IN BUDAPEST, HUNGARY

Viktor Barna won five World Singles Championship titles and was a key member of the Hungarian team that dominated table tennis in the 1930s. Barna also won numerous doubles and team titles, making him one of the most successful players in the history of the sport.

THE PIONEER OF WORLD PING-PONG

Viktor Barna is famous for being one of the pioneers of table tennis internationally. His technique, innovative style of play and dominance on the world stage in the 1930s contributed greatly to popularizing the sport. Barna was known for his offensive play, his ability to read the game and his exceptional sportsmanship. His contribution to ping pong goes beyond his victories, as he helped transform this recreational sport into a serious and respected competition.

Viktor Barna's career has been marked by historic moments. His dominance at the World Championships, where he won five singles titles, set high standards for future generations. His rivalry with other great players of the era, such as Richard Bergmann, created some legendary matches. Barna also played a crucial role in establishing Hungary as a table tennis superpower in the 1930s. After his sporting retirement, he continued to influence the world of table tennis as an author and promoter of the sport.

Viktor inspired the creation of the Ping-Pong World Cup.

RICHARD BERGMANN

BORN APRIL 10, 1919 IN VIENNA, AUSTRIA

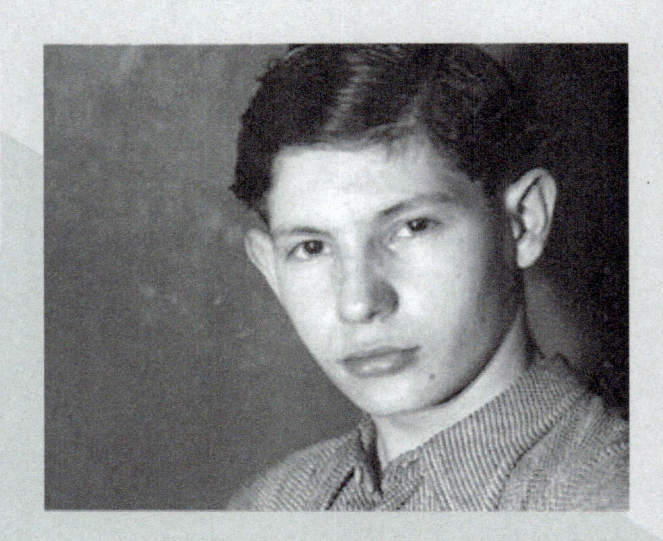

Richard Bergmann won seven World Championship titles, including four in singles and three in doubles, mainly in the 1930s and 1940s. Bergmann was recognized for his defensive style of play, his exceptional cutting technique, and his ability to come back in matches that seemed lost.

THE ORIGINAL MAESTRO OF DEFENSE

Richard Bergmann is famous for his revolutionary defensive style of play and his remarkable longevity at the highest level. His game was characterized by impenetrable defense and an ability to counterattack effectively, making him formidable against even the most aggressive attackers. He is also known for his fighting spirit and his ability to turn around difficult situations, often winning crucial points in spectacular fashion.

Richard Bergmann's career has been punctuated by memorable moments. His victories at the World Championships, particularly in singles, demonstrated his technical and tactical mastery. His rivalry with Viktor Barna, another great player of the era, resulted in legendary duels, contributing to the rise of ping-pong as a competitive sport. Bergmann was also a pioneer in the development of the defensive game, influencing generations of players. His ability to maintain a high level of performance over two decades, despite the disruptions of World War II, is a testament to his determination and love for the sport.

When the Nazis invaded Austria in 1938, Bergmann fled to England. In 1939, he won his second world singles crown and the world doubles title, with Viktor Barna as his partner.

ICHIRO OGIMURA

BORN JUNE 25, 1932 IN ITŌ, JAPAN

Ichiro Ogimura won two world singles titles (1954, 1956) and several other doubles and team titles. Ogimura was a pioneer in his country, establishing Japan as a major force in international table tennis. He was recognized for his fast play, innovative technique and exemplary sportsmanship.

THE VISIONARY OF JAPANESE PING-PONG

Ichiro Ogimura is famous for revolutionizing ping pong in Japan and internationally. His technique, notably his quick footwork and strategic use of topspin, was ahead of his time. Ogimura was not only an exceptional player, but also an ambassador for the sport, helping to popularize ping pong in his native country and across the world.

Ichiro Ogimura's career is marked by several remarkable events. His victories at the World Championships in the 1950s highlighted the talent and innovation of Japanese table tennis. His ability to compete and defeat the best players of the time set new standards for the sport. In addition to his competitive successes, Ogimura played a key role in the training and development of young players, including future world champions. After his playing career, he continued to influence the sport as president of the International Table Tennis Federation.

Ichiro helped introduce the team event to the World Championships.

#22

STELLAN BENGTSSON

Stellan Bengtsson won the World Singles Championship in 1971, becoming the first Swede and the youngest player at the time to win the title. Bengtsson also won several medals at the World Championships in doubles and teams, as well as the European Championships.

THE SWEDISH PING-PONG PIONEER

Stellan Bengtsson is famous for paving the way for Sweden and Europe in table tennis dominated by Asian players. His victory at the 1971 World Championship was a key moment, breaking barriers and showing that European players could excel at a world level. He is recognized for his playing technique, particularly his top-spin game, which was considered innovative at the time.

Stellan Bengtsson's career is punctuated by notable events. Besides his world singles title, he played a vital role in several doubles and team victories, helping Sweden establish themselves as a strong nation in table tennis. His rivalry with other great players of his era resulted in exciting matches, contributing to the evolution of the sport. After his playing career, Bengtsson became a coach, passing on his knowledge and experience to new generations of players.

He was the first Swedish table tennis player to win the individual world championship in 1971.

RYU SEUNG-MIN

BORN AUGUST
5, 1982 IN
SEOUL, SOUTH
KOREA

Ryu Seung-min won the singles gold medal at the 2004 Athens Olympic Games, a memorable performance that made table tennis history. Ryu also contributed to South Korea's successes in team competitions, with notable performances at the World Championships and Asian Championships.

THE OLYMPIC CHAMPION IN THE PENHOLDER GRIP

Ryu Seung-min is famous for his dynamic playing style and his Korean penholder grip, a technique that allowed him to develop a fast and powerful offensive game. His victory at the 2004 Olympic Games was a landmark moment for South Korean table tennis, demonstrating its ability to compete at the highest international level. Ryu is also known for his speed, agility, and ability to perform spectacular returns, making him a favorite among ping pong fans.

Ryu Seung-min's career is marked by several significant achievements. In addition to his Olympic gold medal, he has been a formidable competitor in international competitions, frequently pitting himself against the best Chinese and European players. Ryu has contributed significantly to the success of the South Korean national team in various international competitions. After his retirement as a player, Ryu remained actively involved in table tennis, taking on important roles in sporting organizations, including as a member of the International Olympic Committee, contributing to the continued evolution of the sport.

After his retirement he got involved in the various international table tennis organizations. He is notably a member of the IOC, president of the Korean Table Tennis Association (KTTA) and president of the COA Entourage Committee.

JORGEN PERSSON

World singles champion in 1991, Jörgen Persson played a crucial role in the golden age of Swedish table tennis. Persson also won several doubles and team medals at the World Championships and European Championships. His longevity in the sport is exceptional, having competed in seven consecutive Olympic Games.

THE LIVING LEGEND OF SWEDISH PING-PONG

Jörgen Persson is famous for his major contribution to the golden era of Swedish table tennis. His victory in the World Singles Championship in 1991 was a landmark moment, establishing Sweden as a major table tennis power. Persson is recognized for his attacking style of play, skillful technique and ability to compete with the world's best players over several decades.

Jörgen Persson's career is punctuated by memorable moments. Besides his world title in 1991, he was a centerpiece of the Swedish teams that challenged China's dominance in the 1980s and 1990s. Persson also set a remarkable record by appearing in seven consecutive Olympic Games, from 1988 to 2012 , proving his consistency and dedication to the sport. His rivalry with players like Jan-Ove Waldner and the great Chinese champions marked the history of ping-pong and helped popularize the sport in Europe.

Jörgen has competed in seven consecutive Olympic Games in table tennis.

KENTA MATSUDAIRA

BORN ON APRIL 11, 1991 IN NANAO, ISHIKAWA, JAPAN

Kenta Matsudaira has won several titles in international tournaments, including the ITTF Opens. Matsudaira is also known for his impressive doubles and team performances, contributing to the success of the Japanese national team in various international competitions.

THE SERVICE VIRTUOSO IN MODERN PING-PONG

Kenta Matsudaira is famous for his unique and innovative serve, often described as one of the most impressive and effective in the world of modern ping pong. His style of play combines agility, precise technique and excellent tactical sense. Matsudaira also stands out for his ability to execute spectacular shots, making him a very entertaining player to watch.

Kenta Matsudaira's career has been marked by several notable events. Her performances in the team and doubles competitions were particularly impressive, showing her ability to work in harmony with her teammates. Matsudaira also had remarkable victories against some of the best players in the world, proving his ability to compete at the highest level. His contribution to the development of ping pong in Japan, through his performances and style of play, was significant, inspiring many young players.

Kenta Matsudaira is known for his unique and effective 'tomahawk' serve.

26

AI FUKUHARA, "AI-CHAN"

BORN NOVEMBER 1, 1988 IN SENDAI, MIYAGI, JAPAN

Ai Fukuhara has won several medals in international competitions, including a team silver medal at the 2012 Olympic Games and a team bronze medal at the 2016 Games. Fukuhara also had a successful career in the ITTF Opens and the World Championships.

THE SHINING STAR OF JAPANESE PING PONG

Ai Fukuhara is famous for being a ping pong prodigy from a young age, captivating Japanese and international audiences with his precocious talent. His dynamic playing style, characterized by quick reflexes and great precision, as well as his endearing personality, have contributed to his popularity. Fukuhara also played an important role in popularizing ping pong in Japan, inspiring many young players.

Ai Fukuhara's career has been marked by several key moments. Her participation in the Olympic Games at the age of 15 made her one of the youngest players to compete at this level. His consistent performances in international competitions have solidified his reputation as a top athlete. Fukuhara has also been an ambassador for table tennis, playing a key role in establishing sporting relations between Japan and other countries, particularly China. Her commitment to sport and her ability to break cultural barriers have made her an iconic figure.

Exceptionally precocious, she began playing table tennis at the age of three and turned professional at ten, which was a record at the time.

27

LI XIAOXIA

BORN JANUARY 16, 1988 IN ANSHAN, LIAONING, CHINA

Li Xiaoxia won the singles gold medal at the 2012 London Olympics and was a key figure in the Chinese team that won team gold in London and Rio in 2016. Li also experienced a considerable success at the World Championships, winning singles, doubles and team titles.

THE SILENT EMPRESS OF THE OLYMPIC TABLE

Li Xiaoxia is famous for her dominant presence in world women's table tennis, particularly for her singles victory at the 2012 Olympic Games. She is notable for her aggressive play, her ability to dominate opponents with powerful shots, and her stability under pressure. Li is also recognized for her ability to execute complex strategies, combining impeccable technique with keen tactical sense, making her formidable in competition.

Li Xiaoxia's career has been punctuated by remarkable moments. Besides her Olympic triumph, she played a crucial role in maintaining China's dominance in women's table tennis. His victories at the World Championships, both in singles and team events, demonstrated his versatility and importance within the Chinese national team. Her rivalry with other great players, like Ding Ning, contributed to some of the most captivating matches in women's ping pong history. After a successful playing career, Li became an inspiration for future generations of female players.

Li Xiaoxia won every major title in a span of two years (2011-2013).

GUO YAN

BORN JUNE 24, 1982 IN BAODING, HEBEI, CHINA

Guo Yan was a formidable competitor at the World Championships, winning several medals in singles, doubles, and teams. Guo has also achieved significant success in ITTF Opens and Asian competitions. Known for her offensive play and her ability to quickly adapt to her opponents.

THE UNDISPUTED STAR OF PING-PONG WITHOUT AN OLYMPIC CROWN

Guo Yan is famous for her consistent and dominant presence in international women's table tennis. She stands out for her offensive style of play, her precise technique, and her ability to execute complex strategies in matches. Guo has been a pillar of the Chinese national team, contributing to its continued success on the international stage.

Guo Yan's career is punctuated by many notable events. His performances at the World Championships and other major competitions showed his technical and tactical excellence. She was a key member of the Chinese team, contributing to several important victories in team competitions. His longevity in the sport, remaining competitive at a high level for many years, is also notable. Guo is recognized for her determination and commitment to ping pong, which has made her a respected and admired figure in the sport.

Guo Yan topped the world rankings without winning an Olympic title.

JIANG JIALIANG

Jiang Jialiang has won the World Singles Championship twice, a remarkable performance that demonstrates his exceptional talent. Jiang also contributed to the Chinese team's successes in international competitions, including winning medals in doubles and team events.

THE INCARNATE DYNAMISM OF CHINESE PING-PONG

Jiang Jialiang is famous for his dynamic playing style and dominant presence in international table tennis during the 1980s. His World Singles Championship victories not only cemented his reputation as an elite player, but also contributed to China's continued dominance in sports.

Jiang Jialiang's career is punctuated by memorable moments and significant victories. His two world singles titles are the highlights of his career, highlighting his technical and tactical superiority. In addition to his individual exploits, Jiang played a crucial role in the Chinese team's performance, providing experience and leadership. His rivalry with other great players of the time, such as Waldner and Boll, led to exciting matches and marked the history of ping pong.

Jiang Jialiang was elected to the Table Tennis Hall of Fame in 2001.

30

JEAN-PHILIPPE GATIEN
"THE MAGICIAN"

BORN OCTOBER
16, 1968 IN
ALÈS, FRANCE

Jean-Philippe Gatien won the singles silver medal at the 1992 Olympic Games in Barcelona, a remarkable feat for a European player at that time. Gatien was also world singles champion in 1993 and won several European singles and doubles titles.

THE BRILLIANCE OF FRENCH PING-PONG ON THE WORLD STAGE

Jean-Philippe Gatien is famous for bringing French ping-pong to a world level. His Olympic silver medal in 1992 and world championship in 1993 were key moments, proving that non-Asian players could excel in the sport. Gatien was known for his tactical approach to the game, combining technique, speed and playing intelligence.

Jean-Philippe Gatien's career is marked by victories and exceptional performances. His world championship victory in 1993 was a historic achievement, placing him among the elites of world table tennis. Gatien was also a key member of the French national team, contributing to several successes in team competitions. His impact on the sport in France was immense, inspiring a generation of players and contributing to the popularization of ping pong in the country.

Jean-Philippe was made a knight of the Legion of Honor in January 2017.

31

WERNER SCHLAGER

BORN SEPTEMBER 28, 1972 IN WIENER NEUSTADT, AUSTRIA

His moment of glory was winning the World Singles Championship in 2003, a rare feat for a non-Asian player in the sport's modern era. Schlager also won several European singles, doubles and team titles. His unpredictable style of play and excellent tactical sense have earned him a reputation as a formidable player.

THE INGENIOUS STRATEGIST OF EUROPEAN PING-PONG

Werner Schlager is famous for his triumph at the 2003 World Championship, where he surprised the ping pong world by beating several favorites to win the title. His style of play, characterized by a wide variety of moves, a keen tactical sense and an ability to quickly adapt to his opponents, has been the key to his success.

Werner Schlager's career was marked by notable successes. In addition to his world title in 2003, he was a pillar of the Austrian team, contributing to numerous victories in European competitions. His ability to compete with the best Asian and European players has made him one of the most respected players of his generation. Schlager is also known for his psychological approach to the game, using intelligence and strategy to outwit his opponents. After his playing career, he became an influential coach, sharing his knowledge and experience with the new generation of players.

Werner Schlager started playing table tennis at the age of 6.

32

PETER KORBEL

BORN JUNE 6, 1971 IN HAVLÍČKŮV BROD, CZECHOSLOVAKIA (NOW CZECH REPUBLIC)

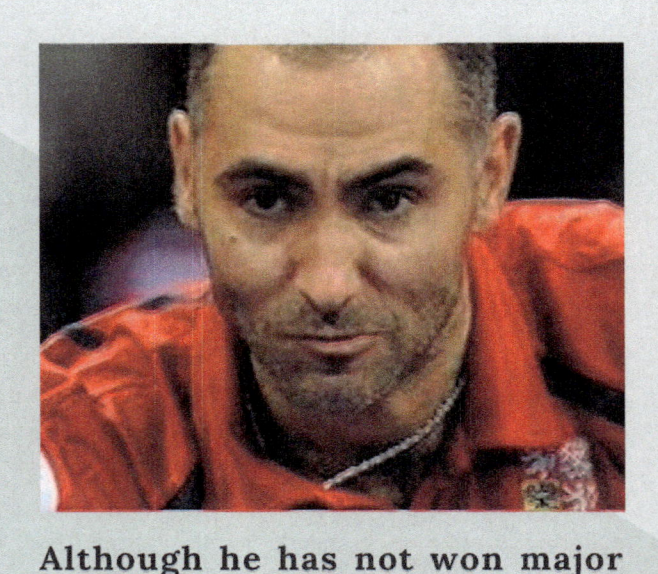

Although he has not won major singles titles, Petr Korbel has been a finalist and medalist in many international tournaments, including the European Championships. His regular participation in high-level competitions and his elegant playing style have earned him great recognition in the world of ping pong.

THE TECHNICAL ELEGANCE OF CZECH PING-PONG

Petr Korbel is famous for his fluid and technical playing style, often considered one of the most elegant in ping pong. He stands out for his excellent forehand, his ability to control the pace of the game, and his intelligent tactical approach. Korbel has been an ambassador of Czech table tennis, representing his country in numerous international competitions and maintaining a constant presence in the top tier of the sport for several years.

Petr Korbel's career has been marked by several important moments. His longevity in the sport, with continued participation in high-level competitions, is particularly remarkable. He has been a fierce competitor in the European Championships, ITTF Opens and other international tournaments, often reaching the final stages and challenging the best players in the world. His ability to maintain a high level of performance over a long period of time has made him a respected figure in table tennis. Outside of his competitive performances, Korbel has been a mentor and role model for young ping pong players, contributing to the development of the sport in his country.

In recognition of his accomplishments and style of play, a ping pong equipment brand named a racket wood in his honor.

33

CHEN JING

BORN SEPTEMBER 20, 1968 IN WUHAN, HUBEI, CHINA

Chen Jing won the singles silver medal at the 1988 Olympic Games in Seoul, representing China. After becoming a naturalized Taiwanese, she also won a bronze medal in singles at the 1996 Olympic Games in Atlanta.

A BRIDGE BETWEEN TWO WORLDS OF PING-PONG

Chen Jing is famous for his unique career that spans two different national ping pong systems. Initially a member of the Chinese team, she later represented Taiwan after her naturalization, a relatively rare and remarkable move in the sport. She is recognized for her powerful playing style and impeccable technique, as well as her ability to remain at the top level of women's ping pong for many years.

Chen Jing's career is marked by success in both China and Taiwan. His transition from one national team to another and his maintenance of high-level performances are unique in the history of ping pong. She was one of the rare players to win Olympic medals under two different flags. Her consistent presence in international competitions and her impact on table tennis in Taiwan, where she helped raise the level of the sport, are also notable.

Chen Jing has won Olympic medals for two different countries.

34

MIKAEL APPELGREN, "THE APPLE"

BORN OCTOBER 15, 1961 IN FALKENBERG, SWEDEN

Mikael Appelgren was a key member of the Swedish team that competed against Chinese dominance in the 1980s and 1990s. Appelgren won several European and world titles, both singles and team. He is particularly recognized for his victories at the European Championships.

THE ARCHITECT OF THE GOLDEN AGE OF SWEDISH PING PONG

Mikael Appelgren is famous for his crucial role in the golden era of Swedish table tennis, helping his country establish itself as a superpower in the sport. He is known for his attacking play, his refined technique and his ability to deliver performances under pressure. His rivalry with Chinese players and Swedish teammates, such as Waldner and Persson, created legendary moments in ping pong history.

Mikael Appelgren's career has been marked by several notable events. His victories at the European Championships and World Championships highlighted his technical mastery and competitive spirit. Appelgren was instrumental in Sweden's historic victories against China, helping to change the dynamics of global table tennis. His style of play, combining power and precision, was admired and imitated by many players. After his playing career he remained involved in table tennis, sharing his experience and knowledge as a coach.

At the age of 40, Mickael Appelgren was still a finalist in the Swedish championships, he also won the veterans' world champion title in 2006.

35

JOHN HILTON

BORN JUNE 25, 1947 IN MANCHESTER, ENGLAND

John Hilton is best known for his incredible victory at the 1980 European Table Tennis Championships in Bern, Switzerland. This victory remains one of the greatest upsets in table tennis history, as Hilton, then relatively unknown at the level, managed to beat much more renowned opponents using an unusual combination of racket rubbers, unsettling the best European players of the time.

THE MAN WHO REVOLUTIONIZED TABLE TENNIS

Using a racket with different rubbers on each side, Hilton unsettled his opponents with varied and unpredictable spins. The victory marked a turning point in European table tennis and inspired many players to rethink their approach to the game. His ability to innovate tactically, combined with his calmness under pressure, made him a fixture in the sport.

Hilton's victory at the 1980 European Championships was one of the most significant events of his career. By defeating top players such as Germany's Jochen Leiß and Sweden's Stellan Bengtsson, Hilton proved that tactical innovation could trump superior technical skills. The tournament also raised questions about the rules governing racket coverings, and shortly thereafter, changes were made to the rules regarding pimpled rackets. His unique approach left a lasting mark on the modern game.

He was using a type of racket that has since been banned.

36

LEE SANG-SU

BORN AUGUST 13, 1990 IN SEOUL, SOUTH KOREA

Lee Sang-su has distinguished himself in numerous international competitions, including the World Championships and the ITTF Opens. Lee won medals in singles, doubles and team events, demonstrating great versatility. His dynamic playing style and excellent technique make him a formidable opponent on the international scene.

THE DYNAMIC POWER OF SOUTH KOREAN PING PONG

Lee Sang-su is famous for his ability to compete with the world's best players, including Chinese players who traditionally dominate the sport. He is known for his speed, his striking power and his aggressiveness in matches. His consistent presence in high-level international competitions and his remarkable performances against top opponents have earned him worldwide recognition.

Lee Sang-su's career is marked by several notable events. His performances at the World Championships, where he reached the final stages in both singles and doubles, show his high technical level and competitiveness. Lee also played a key role in the South Korean team's success, contributing to several important victories in team competitions. He is also known for his energetic and exciting matches, which often captivate spectators and ping pong fans.

He won his first Asian Singles Championships in 2021. This is South Korea's first title in this category of the competition since 1952.

37

HUGO CALDERANO

BORN JUNE 22, 1996 IN RIO DE JANEIRO, BRAZIL

Hugo Calderano has accumulated an impressive track record, including winning titles at the Latin American Championships and distinguishing himself at various ITTF Opens. Calderano also had notable performances at the Olympic Games and World Championships.

THE RISING STAR OF PING-PONG IN LATIN AMERICA

Hugo Calderano is famous for raising Brazilian and Latin American table tennis to an international level. Known for his offensive play, his precise technique and his ability to deliver impressive performances against higher ranked players, he changed the perception of ping pong in the Western Hemisphere. Calderano is particularly appreciated for his work ethic, determination and tactical approach to the game.

Hugo Calderano's career has been marked by several significant moments. He became one of the few non-Asian players to reach the highest ranks of the ITTF world rankings. His performances in major tournaments, including victories against world top players, have proven his competitiveness at the international level. Its presence in major competitions has not only inspired many young players in Latin America, but also helped increase the visibility and popularity of ping pong in the region.

In January 2022, he peaked at number 3 in the world rankings, becoming the greatest player from the Americas of all time.

38

NATALIA PARTYKA

BORN JULY 27, 1989 IN GDAŃSK, POLAND

Born with a birth defect that left her with an incomplete arm, Natalia Partyka won gold medals in class 10 competitions at the 2004, 2008, 2012 and 2016 Paralympic Games. She also competed in the Olympic Games, making She is one of the rare athletes to compete in both the Olympic and Paralympic Games.

BRAVING THE LIMITS IN PING PONG

Natalia Partyka is famous for transcending physical barriers to excel in ping pong at a global level. His participation and success in both the Olympic Games and the Paralympic Games illustrate his incredible talent and determination. Partyka is an inspiration to many athletes, demonstrating that physical limitations can be overcome with passion and dedication.

Natalia Partyka's career is punctuated by remarkable successes and historic moments. His dominance in Paralympic competitions is unprecedented, having won several consecutive gold medals. His participation in the Olympic Games represents a rare and impressive feat, illustrating his exceptional level of skill. She has been a model for sports integration, showing that excellence in sport can transcend conventional categories of competition.

She is again one of the only athletes (along with South African sprinter Oscar Pistorius) to compete in both the 2012 Summer Olympics and Paralympics.

39

LI JIAO

BORN JANUARY 15, 1973 IN QINGDAO, CHINA

Li Jiao won several European Championship singles titles and was a mainstay of the Dutch team in the team competitions. Li also competed in the Olympic Games and had a notable presence in international competitions, competing against the best female players in the world.

THE POWER OF PING-PONG AT THE CROSSROADS OF CULTURES

Li Jiao is famous for her successful transition from the Chinese ping pong system to the European scene, becoming one of Europe's most dominant players. She is known for her aggressive playing style, powerful forehand technique, and ability to compete at a high level well beyond the age when most athletes retire. His career illustrates his ability to adapt and his dedication to the sport.

Li Jiao's career has been marked by many highlights, including his multiple victories at the European Championships, which demonstrated his high technical level and perseverance. His contribution to Dutch and European table tennis is significant, with outstanding performances in team and individual competitions.
Furthermore, his longevity in the sport, remaining competitive at a high level despite age, is a testament to his exceptional passion and fitness.

Li Jiao competed in four consecutive Olympic Games for the Netherlands.

40

KIM TAEK-SOO

BORN MAY 25, 1970 IN INCHEON, SOUTH KOREA

Although he did not win an Olympic medal in singles, Kim Taek-soo was a key competitor in doubles and teams, winning medals at the Olympic Games and World Championships. Kim was also a dominant player in Asian competitions, with several titles to his name.

THE SOUTH KOREAN MAESTRO OF PEN HOLDER

Kim Taek-soo is famous for his dynamic playing style and his mastery of the penholder grip, a technique often associated with Asian players. He was a leading player in South Korean table tennis in the 1990s, helping to establish South Korea as a major nation in the sport. His speed, his ability to generate powerful offensive shots, and his fighting spirit have made him a feared opponent on the international scene.

Kim Taek-soo's career has been marked by impressive doubles and team performances, including at the Olympic Games and World Championships. He played a crucial role in the South Korean team's victories, demonstrating his importance in both doubles and team competition. Following his playing career, Kim became an influential coach, helping to cultivate the new generation of South Korean players and continuing to have a significant impact on table tennis.

In 2010, he was announced would succeed Yoo Nam-Kyu as head coach of the South Korea national table tennis team.

WANG CHUQIN

Wang Chuqin has won several important titles, including junior competitions and ITTF Opens. Wang showed his potential by winning medals in various international tournaments and contributing to the Chinese team's success in team competitions.

THE RISE OF A NEW STAR IN CHINESE PING-PONG

Wang Chuqin is famous for his rapid rise through the table tennis ranks, both domestically and internationally. He is known for his powerful playing style and excellent forehand, as well as his ability to compete with more experienced players. His performances in international competitions, notably the ITTF Opens, have highlighted his potential and ability to become one of the leading players in world table tennis.

Wang Chuqin's career, although relatively short so far, is already marked by notable events. His victories in international junior competitions and impressive performances in professional tournaments have shown that he is a player to watch. His contribution to the Chinese team's victories in international competitions has also been notable, highlighting his growing importance within the national team. His matches against the world's best players were key moments, demonstrating his talent and competitiveness.

He is the first Chinese player born after the year 2000 to participate in the China Table Tennis Super League competition, in 2015.

42

LIN GAOYUAN

BORN MARCH 19, 1995 IN SHENZHEN, GUANGDONG, CHINA

Lin Gaoyuan distinguished himself in several ITTF Opens, winning singles and doubles titles. Lin was also a key part of the Chinese team in team competitions, contributing to numerous victories. His refined technique, his fast game and his powerful forehand place him among the best players in the world.

THE NEW WAVE OF SUPREMACY IN CHINESE PING-PONG

Lin Gaoyuan is famous for his rapid rise and his ability to compete with the big names in world table tennis. He is known for his dynamic playing style, exceptional speed and ability to execute difficult shots with precision. Lin represents the new generation of Chinese players, continuing China's tradition of supremacy in sports.

Lin Gaoyuan's career has been marked by outstanding performances in international tournaments. He has won several ITTF Opens in singles and doubles, proving his versatility and skill. Lin also played a crucial role in the Chinese team's victories, particularly in the World Championships and team competitions. His matches against other top players were often highlights, demonstrating his potential to become one of the best players in ping pong history.

He acquired his first international singles title at the age of 22 by winning gold at the 2017 Asian Cup.

43

GAO NING

BORN OCTOBER 11, 1982 IN LIAONING, CHINA

Gao Ning has spearheaded the Singapore team in numerous international competitions, winning several medals at the Commonwealth Games and Asian Championships. Gao also participated in the Olympic Games, where he displayed strong performances.

THE DRIVING FORCE OF SINGAPOREAN PING-PONG

Gao Ning is famous for being the mainstay of the Singapore national team for many years, leading the team to notable successes on the international stage. His solid technique, consistency and ability to perform under pressure have greatly contributed to his individual success and that of his team.

Gao Ning's career is dotted with notable moments. His multiple medals at the Commonwealth Games and Asian Championships are testament to his consistency and high level of play. His ability to compete and achieve victories against world-renowned players has made him a respected figure in the world of ping pong. Gao also played a crucial role in Singapore's rise to prominence in world table tennis, particularly in team competitions.

Gao Ning's best place in the ITTF world rankings was 9th, which he reached in April 2008.

44

ZORAN PRIMORAC

BORN MAY 10, 1969 IN ZADAR, CROATIA

Zoran Primorac has won several medals in international competitions, including a silver medal in doubles at the 1988 Olympic Games in Seoul. Primorac also distinguished himself at the World Championships and the European Championships, making him one of the most respected European players of his era.

A PIONEER OF CROATIAN PING-PONG ON THE WORLD STAGE

Zoran Primorac is famous for his significant impact on table tennis, not only in Croatia but also internationally. He is recognized for his refined technique, offensive play and ability to compete at the highest level for several decades. Primorac is also admired for his longevity in the sport and his role as a pioneer of table tennis in the Balkans.

Zoran Primorac's career is marked by exceptional performances at the Olympic Games, World Championships and European Championships. He played a crucial role in the introduction and popularization of ping pong in Croatia, inspiring many generations of players. His consistent presence in high-level competitions for almost three decades is a testament to his skill and determination.

Zoran Primorac has competed in seven consecutive Olympic Games in table tennis.

45

SEIYA KISHIKAWA

BORN MAY 21, 1987 IN KITAKYŪSHŪ, JAPAN

Although he has not won any major singles titles, Seiya Kishikawa has been a consistent competitor in team and doubles competitions. Kishikawa contributed to the Japanese team's successes in the World Championships and ITTF Opens, gaining recognition for his dynamic playing style and coordination in doubles.

JAPANESE PRECISION IN DOUBLES AND TEAMS

Seiya Kishikawa is famous for his doubles expertise and his crucial role in team competitions. Known for his precision and impeccable timing, he formed effective doubles partnerships, distinguishing himself in international tournaments. Kishikawa is appreciated for his tactical play and his ability to adapt to the different styles of his opponents, which has made him an important part of the Japanese team.

Seiya Kishikawa's career is marked by significant contributions to the Japanese team's success in international competitions. His doubles performances, particularly his partnerships with other top Japanese players, were particularly notable. Kishikawa also played a key role in the team competitions, helping Japan achieve impressive results at the World Championships and other major tournaments. His consistent and reliable presence in high-level competitions has underlined his importance in Japanese table tennis.

He is recognized for his exceptional coordination in doubles.

46

JHA'S CHILD

BORN JUNE 19, 2000 IN MILPITAS, CALIFORNIA, UNITED STATES

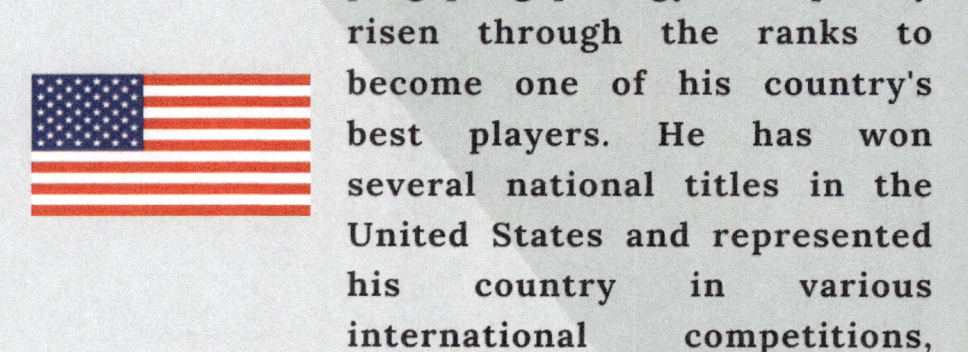

Kanak Jha, a young American ping pong prodigy, has quickly risen through the ranks to become one of his country's best players. He has won several national titles in the United States and represented his country in various international competitions, including the Olympic Games.

THE FACE OF THE NEW GENERATION OF AMERICAN PING-PONG

Kanak Jha is famous for being one of the youngest players to represent the United States in high-level international ping pong competitions. His rapid rise, refined technique and maturity in the game set him apart among his peers. Jha is also known for his attacking style of play and his ability to compete with more experienced and higher ranked players.

Kanak Jha's career is marked by several notable events from a young age. He was the youngest player to represent the United States in the Olympics in table tennis and won national titles by defeating older, experienced opponents. Jha has also performed well in international competitions, which is a testament to his potential to become one of the leading players in global table tennis in the years to come.

He was banned from all competitions for 1 year for failing to pass three anti-doping controls. This suspension starts on December 1, 2022 and lasts until December 1, 2023.

47

KOKI NIWA

BORN OCTOBER 10, 1994 IN TOMAKOMAI, HOKKAIDO, JAPAN

His record includes medals at the World Championships and the Asian Championships, in both singles and doubles. Koki Niwa also participated in the Olympic Games, where he competed at a high level. Known for his fast play, refined technique and powerful forehand, Niwa has earned a reputation for excellence in international table tennis.

THE FUSION OF SPEED AND TECHNIQUE IN JAPANESE PING PONG

Koki Niwa is famous for his exceptional speed and precise technique, which make him a formidable opponent. His style of play, combining speed, agility and creative shots, sets him apart in international competitions. Niwa is also known for his ability to execute difficult shots with ease, making him spectacular to watch and feared by his opponents.

Koki Niwa's career is marked by impressive performances in both singles and doubles. He won medals at the World and Asian Championships, asserting his position as one of Japan's best players. His clashes with the world's best players, particularly those from China and Europe, have often been highlights of his career, highlighting his talent and competitiveness at the highest level of ping pong.

He beat world champions while still a teenager.

48

TOMOKAZU HARIMOTO
"WONDER KID"

BORN JUNE 27, 2003 IN SENDAI, MIYAGI, JAPAN

Tomokazu Harimoto broke several youth records, becoming the youngest winner of an ITTF World Tour tournament. Harimoto has also won medals in major international competitions, including the ITTF World Championships and Opens.

THE TEENAGE PHENOMENON OF JAPANESE PING-PONG

Tomokazu Harimoto is famous for his outstanding achievements at an incredibly young age. He broke records by becoming the youngest player to win major titles in table tennis, showing a maturity and technique that defied his age. Harimoto is known for his attacking style of play, his incredible speed and his ability to execute powerful shots.

Tomokazu Harimoto's career is notable for his many early successes. He set records as the youngest winner in several ITTF tournaments and consistently challenged and beat much more experienced world-class players. His performances in competitions such as the ITTF World Championships and Opens have been widely praised, affirming his status as one of the most promising talents in world table tennis.

At the 2016 World Championships, he was the youngest Junior World Champion of all time with his victory in singles and won, in addition to team Gold, the silver medal in doubles.

49

LIU SHIWEN

BORN APRIL 12, 1991 IN LIAONING, CHINA

Liu Shiwen has won several singles and doubles titles at the World Championships, as well as the ITTF Opens. Liu is also an Olympic medalist, having contributed to several victories for the Chinese team in team competitions. She is considered one of the best ping pong players of her generation.

THE BRILLIANCE AND PRECISION OF CHINESE WOMEN'S PING-PONG

Liu Shiwen is famous for her dominance in women's ping pong, particularly in singles competitions where she shone with her fast and precise playing style. She is known for her ability to execute technical shots with great speed, which has earned her numerous titles. His consistency and excellence in international competitions make him an emblematic figure of ping-pong.

Liu Shiwen's career is marked by many key moments. His victories at the World Championships and his performances in the ITTF Opens demonstrate his technical and tactical superiority. She played a crucial role in the Chinese team's success in team competitions, including the Olympic Games. Her rivalry with other top players has often been at the heart of memorable matches, underscoring her status as a top competitor.

She holds the record for World Cup victories. She won 5 editions. At 18 she won her first title in 2009.

50

CHEN QI

BORN APRIL 15, 1984 IN NANTONG, JIANGSU, CHINA

Chen Qi is known for winning the men's doubles gold medal at the 2004 Olympic Games in Athens, partnering Ma Lin. Chen has also been a key member of the Chinese team in international competitions, winning titles at the World Championships in doubles and teams.

AN IMPOSING FORCE IN DOUBLE OLYMPIC PING-PONG

Chen Qi is famous for his major contribution to the success of the Chinese ping pong team, especially in the doubles and team events. His talent for doubles play, combined with his ability to perform powerful and precise shots, was essential in his Olympic and world victories. Chen is also recognized for his fighting spirit and constant commitment to maintaining a high level of performance.

Chen Qi's career is punctuated by several highlights, including his doubles victory at the 2004 Olympic Games and his multiple world titles. These achievements highlight his skill and mastery in high-level competitions.

Furthermore, his role in the Chinese team's continued dominance on the world stage has been crucial. Chen consistently competed against and beat some of the best players in the world, cementing his reputation as one of the great players of his era.

Chen Qi began receiving training at Nantong Spare-time Sports School in 1990, at the age of 6. He became a member of the provincial team at the age of 12.

As we conclude our journey through "The 50 Legends of Table Tennis", we are left with a deep admiration for these extraordinary athletes.

Their dedication, passion and competitive spirit are not only an inspiration to table tennis players, but also a powerful reminder of what commitment and perseverance can achieve.

These stories are not just those of victory and defeat, but also tales of innovation, resilience and human excellence.

As we close this book, the echoes of these legends will continue to inspire and influence the world of table tennis for generations to come.

Share with us your reactions after discovering or rediscovering these 50 legends
Visit us on our networks: